ADOPTION:

THE
UNKNOWN
BLESSING

ADOPTION:

THE
UNKNOWN
BLESSING

ReGina R. Smithwick

Editorial Midwife Publishing

Ordering Information
Quantity sales. On quantity purchases by corporations, associations, and others—orders by trade bookstores and wholesalers, contact ReGina Smithwick at smithwicksolutions@gmail.com

EDITORIAL SERVICES
Lita P. Ward, the Editorial Midwife
LPW Editing & Consulting Services, LLC
www.litapward.com

Published in the United States of America

ISBN: 978-0-578-89100-2

DEDICATION

I would like to dedicate this book to the four people that made me possible: Patricia Ann Morton, Nathaniel Daniels Jr., Doris F. Smithwick, and Hildria Franco Smithwick. God spoke to you, and I am glad you listened. Through you, I was blessed four times.

ACKNOWLEDGMENTS

To my children Regina, Franklin Jr., and Dillon: You are the reason I do all. If you put your mind to it, you can do anything. Can you believe your mommy is now an author?

I also would like to thank the best families in the world: The Nobles and Smithwicks. They loved me unconditionally and never treated me any differently. That means the world to me. Love you all.

To my amazing siblings: Terresa Morton Reese, Anthony Morton, Natalie Daniels, Monique Daniels, Nathaniel Daniels III, and Brittany Simone Daniels.

The Morton's and Daniels family

To the people who helped me on this journey: Rev. Melissa M. Nobles, Lorie Jones Chatman, Pia Y. Staine, Yolanda T. Richey, Tonya B. Jones, Tara Wright, Monique Barnes, Carla Lynn Morgan, Tiffany Cunningham, Terri Booker, Sharon T. Elder, Shannon McGuire-Lee, Shabara Janelle Jenkins, Joy Renee Brown, Andrea Collins-White, and Joseph John Mann

TABLE OF CONTENTS

CHAPTER ONE
I DID MY WORK

My Breakdown & Breakthrough

In September 2019, it started as a regular Saturday. I ran some errands and cleaned my house. I had a date that evening to meet this guy for the first time. I made it to the restaurant; as we were sitting there eating dinner, I knew this would not work. I knew this weeks ago; however, I wanted to make sure and did not want to judge him before we met. However, as I continue, you will see why this was not the right way to handle this situation. After the date, I was told how he liked me a lot, I was so pretty, and he wanted to see how this would go.

Later that evening, I received a call from him to let me know he did not have that tingly feeling he usually had when he knows that she is the one. Add insult to injury, he spoke to his uncle, and he told him he should not date me because he did not have that feeling. I was speechless, seeing he just told me he liked me. After that conversation, I hung up the phone and just started to cry because I allowed his judgment to change my mood and doubt myself. The worst part of this is I was going to defend myself to prove I am a good person. This made me look inside and ask why? I felt horrible and cried myself to sleep. But, I would like to thank my friend and sorority sister Shabara Jenkins for checking on me that life-changing night.

I kept thinking, though. I am a good person, and I have great qualities. However, why didn't he see that? I knew I had to find out why I felt this way and break this unending cycle of handling rejection. I needed help at this point. I needed to do something different to get different results. I did not want to go into my 50's with this problem. I wanted to free myself and stand in my truth.

Seeking Help

I woke up the next day feeling better, knowing I was going to do something about my situation. I prayed and asked God to guide my path on this uncharted territory. In the black community seeing a therapist or a life coach is a stigma. I love my Lord and Savior, and I believe He places the gift of helping people in therapists and life coaches. He puts them on this earth to help people like me. I knew I wanted a person that specializes in theory and spiritual practices. This is especially important to me; therefore, I needed God at the forefront of this journey.

As I began to conduct my research, I wanted a black female therapist, if possible.

I believed I would feel more comfortable being vulnerable with sharing personal information about me that I normally do not do. I remember that a friend of mine used a person that she recommended. I reach out to her and set up a consultation. From day one, I was so comfortable she understood what I was feeling and implemented a 13-week plan for us to follow. Seeing she lives in New York and I am in North Carolina, we utilized the conference call method. Part of the plan was to promise that I would commit to the process and to be present. Plus, I had to purchase a book called *30-Day Mental Diet: The Way To a Better Life* by Willis Kinnear. So, anxiously I set a date to get started.

I knew this would not be easy. And like the old folks say, "A hit dog will holler," and I would be hollering a lot during this process. However, I was ready to change, and I was tired of being sick and tired. I had to get to the core and stand in my truth. By any means necessary, I wanted this cycle to finally end.

When the day finally arrived, I started my first day with my life coach, not knowing what to expect. However, I was open and ready to do my work. We spoke on what I expected to accomplish and what she expected from me: determination, openness, and dedication. I made the commitment to her and, most importantly, to myself.

The first session was eye-opening and scary because I knew that I was about to see the real ReGina. There would be no smiling and laughing my way through this one. After the session, I started reading the *30-day Mental Diet*. Before reading, I did not know my place in the universe or that I was important. As I continued to read, I realized I made a difference, and I have a purpose in this world. I have to say this book has changed my life! It made me think about why I am here, as it developed dedication and consistency in my journey.

Working On My Insecurities

In the process of doing my work, I realize I had more issues than I thought, and I needed to face them head-on. I reached out to the life coach about my breakdown because of the hurt and rejection I felt because someone did not like me. He did not validate me or make me feel valuable. However, the most important issues were why did I feel this way? And why did I allow a person I barely knew to change my mood so much or so quickly?

To obtain a full understanding and clarity, I needed to dig deeper and start from the beginning. I was the person everyone liked, and I always liked everyone. I was everyone's friend and a people pleaser; but, I never knew why. As I dug deeper, I learned this commenced in 1977 when my parents told me I was **adopted**.

It was a Saturday morning around noon because I could remember Soul Train was on the television. They sat me down and told me I was loved, and my birth mother gave me up to have a better life. At the time, I thought I was good, and I just continued to play. However, that was the start of my insecurities. As I grew older, my senses were heightened with anyone mentioning the word *adoption*.

Over the years, I heard people say, "You must be adopted because you are different," or jokingly say, "You are loved less than the other siblings." I just decided not to tell anyone because I thought people would see me less than or use it against me. Of course, my adopted family never treated me differently. They loved me just like I was born into the family. As a matter of fact, they never mentioned it or told anyone outside the family. Therefore, I thank the Nobles and Smithwick families for never making me feel less than.

I recall one situation, and my adoption was used negatively when my status was told without my permission. However, after I thought about it, I admit that I gave it too much power by hiding my adoption from the world. Basically, I gave the person the bullets to shoot me with my own gun called insecurity. From this revelation, I decided for my 50th birthday to confront my issue and finally show the world who I was. May I introduce myself?

My name is ReGina R. Smithwick

and

I am adopted!

*About **135,000** children are adopted in the United States each year. Of non- stepparent adoptions, about **59%** are from the child welfare (or foster) system, **26%** are from other countries, and **15%** are voluntarily relinquished American babies.*

(https://adoptionnetwork.com/adoption-myths-facts/domestic-us-statistics/)

CHAPTER TWO
ADOPTION

My Birth Parents

The definition of adoption is "the action or fact of legally taking another person's child, and bringing it up as one's own." So adoption is a great thing to do, right? Morally, you are saving a child from being an orphan or in the foster care system. However, adoption has many sides.

Let's discuss my birth parents. My birth parents met in the late '60s in Danville,

Virginia. Only teenagers, they developed a special bond during their on-and-off-again relationship. My birth father followed my mother to Washington, D.C., and New York, having a good time experiencing life. During their relationship, she was also involved with another special person, and two children were born. Nevertheless, my dad remained in the picture.

In September of 1969, I was conceived. My parents broke up, and he went back to Danville, not knowing she was pregnant with me. Now, my 20-year-old mother was left with a decision. No one will ever know what she thought; however, I can imagine it was a lot to deal with. In my search, I obtained some paperwork from the State of New York that included a personal statement about why she had to give me up. It states she was unemployed, on public assistance, and had two children already. She was trying to go back to school and find employment and did not know how that could happen with a third child.

I remember being 20 years old and the decisions I made. Most of them were not the greatest. Therefore, I can honestly say I totally understand what my birth mother did and had to do. I am neither mad nor upset. I believe she did the best she could in the situation she was in. Without telling anyone besides her best friend, she decided to give me up for adoption.

Let's walk through the mental process of how you can carry a life in your belly for nine months and know you were not going to keep him or her. Imagine feeling the kicking and movement of your child, knowing you would have to give your child away. You take care of yourself to make sure you have a healthy baby to give him or her a fighting chance. This had to have been one of the hardest things she ever had to do. Nevertheless, she made a very mature decision. She made the ultimate sacrifice to show and give unconditional love to someone she had not met and would not raise.

On Wednesday, June 3, 1970, on a summer day in Harlem, Patricia Ann Morton gave birth to a queen named ReGina, which means queen. She spent three days with me and then gave me to the adoption agency. During those precious three days, I always wondered what she said to me. After talking to my new family, I know she was a woman of God, so I have a feeling she prayed over me.

Mom, I can never say it enough...
Thank you for showing me the meaning of
unconditional love.

From the small city of Plymouth, North Carolina, my adopted parents met in the eighth grade and were high school sweethearts. When they graduated, they moved to New York. After getting settled, they were married in 1963. My mother was unable to birth children naturally; however, they had love to give. My parents came from large families; my mother was one of 17 children, and my dad has 11 siblings. So it was established from the gate that they would not have a lot of children. Most couples in the '60s and '70s had children early, but my parents were 27 and 28 when they adopted me. They did their research and found a wonderful agency in Westchester County, N.Y. This was new territory, uncharted waters, since my parents were the first in their family to adopt using outside sources. I am grateful that they thought outside the box with their decision. I asked my mommy if she spoke to anyone about the decision to adopt. She said, "No, your father and I made the decision. Once it was confirmed, we told the family."

After I was born, the agency contacted my soon-to-be parents stating they had a baby they would love and come down to the agency. When they arrived at the agency, and my parents saw me for the first time, Mommy said I smiled at them. They knew right then I was their daughter. They were told that my birth mother named me ReGina; however, they could change my name if they wanted to. Because my mommy is a great person, she said, "No, I want her to keep that connection. Plus, she looks like a ReGina." Lovingly, she gave me a middle name. Once again, that is the expression of unconditional love, even before they took me home.

The Good, Bad and Ugly
Of Adoption

I n my experience, there are three parts of adoption. Being adopted is a mixed bag of emotions and feelings, and those things can change during your lifetime. I am here to tell you that it is okay to feel differently because being adopted is not a cookie-cutter. Every situation is different, and how the adopted parents handle it can make a difference as well.

The good is that God matches you with a family, so you won't have to be raised as an orphan. You will be raised in a home with plenty of love. You have a chance to become something great and make a mark in this world. I believe adopted children were picked twice by God. First, by your birth parents and again by your adopted parents. We have double the blessings!

However, the bad is you may not know where you came from. No one in your family looks like you. And even though you do pick up some of your adopted family traits, there are some mannerisms that you can't explain. I always wondered what my birth mother was doing? Did she think about me on my birthday? Did I have any siblings? Where is my birth father? So many unanswered questions. As I got older and started to go to the doctor on my own, they would ask me if I have a history in my family of different illnesses and conditions. Unfortunately, I had to tell them I don't know because I am adopted. Believe it or not, I was kind of embarrassed. Although being adopted was not my fault, it is how I felt. I do think it's important to find your birth parents just for the medical history alone. It's good to know how you can avoid certain conditions if you can.

Well, my ugly was the stigma I placed around being adopted and why I kept it a secret for so long. When I was younger, I overheard kids say to their siblings, "You are not really our brother! You must be adopted." Or the other familiar statement was, "Yeah, you are different; you must be adopted." Although they might have played around and joked about it, I began to think that being adopted was bad and to feel ashamed about it. When I was a teenager, people started asking me where I got my height from, seeing I was taller than my parents. However, everyone said I looked just like my daddy. Well, you know what they say, "If you feed someone long enough, they start looking like you."

This was the beginning of the snowball effect. I did not want people to use this against me, tease me, or see me as less than a person because I was raised without my birth parents. More importantly, I did not want anyone to look at my parents differently. So I decided to not tell anyone.

Fortunately, at 49 years old, I realized that the problem was not me; others used this information against me because they were not happy with themselves. I had no control over being adopted, and I should not be ashamed about four people loving me unconditionally. Without a doubt, I was unknowingly blessed.

Now, to the best part, the empowerment. I know every adopted child does not feel the same as me. Some would like to keep things the way they are and not rock the boat. However, suppose you want to find your parents and are scared of what your adopted family would think or say. Ladies and gentlemen, in that case, you can't worry about that. This is something you have to do for YOU and YOU only! They are not in your shoes and don't know how it feels to not know where you come from. If you get some resistance, it's not because they don't want the best for you. This is very uncomfortable for them as well.

In most cases, they may feel that you will leave them for your new family, and that's not the case. You do not have to choose between both. When you are adopted and locate new family members, you just have more family to love.

"In short: Placing a child for adoption is not "giving up on" or "giving away" your child. It's making the brave, selfless choice to do what is best for both of you — and it's one to be commended."

McLaughlin SD, Manninen DL, Winges LD, Do Adolescents Who Relinquish Their Children Fare Better or Worse Than Those Who Raise Them? Family Planning Perspectives, 20:1 (Jan. - Feb. 1998), pp. 25-32

CHAPTER THREE

MY NEW FAMILY

How Did The Connection Happen?

Before I tell you this part of my story, I believe in divine order, and everything happens for a reason. Things in your life happen when it is supposed to happen, not a minute too soon. When I started my journey to locate my birth mother, I knew I had to tell my two best friends that I was adopted. I trust my life with Yolanda and Pia, so that decision was not a hard one. Even though they were shocked, they were also very supportive, which I expected.

In 2002 I decided to go to Harlem Hospital in Harlem, N.Y., where I was born to find my birth mother's name. One of my best friends, Pia, came with me for support. Tightly, I held onto my birth certificate and social security card. I did not know where to go; however, I stopped the first employee I saw and told her what I was there to do. This may have sounded like a simple task, right? But just imagine how difficult this must have been for someone who had never said out loud to a stranger that she was adopted. Graciously, the employee guided me to the records department, where one lady was working behind the desk. I gave her my information and asked if she could tell me what women gave birth on June 3, 1970. This was when God stepped in. She was not supposed to tell me; however, she matched my birth certificate number to the original birth certificate and found my birth mother's name. She wrote her name and the address of where my mother lived at the time of my birth on a form and gave it to me. I was so emotional that I had my birth mother's name, Patricia Ann Morton! It was an amazing feeling just to know the name of the person who gave birth to me.

When I arrived back home, I began my in-depth research. Believe it or not, my birth mother's name was popular in New York. However, in her paperwork, I spotted information about Virginia. Remember this part, and it will make sense later in the book.

With the information I had, I wrote the State of New York to get additional information. Surprisingly, weeks later, they mailed me a statement that Patricia had written to the adoption agency. It was emotional to see her handwriting and read her words. She explained why she put me up for adoption, and some background about her journey. From the statement, I knew I had two siblings, my birth father's age and that he was black. At that point, I wanted to find her even more.

There was a show on TLC about a woman who united adopted children to their birth parents. At the end of the show, she provided her contact information. So I reached out to her, and we actually spoke on the phone. She was excited to assist me on my journey in finding my birth mother. There was one problem: her rate was $2,500. Remember, this was 2002 or 2003, and we did not have the DNA kits like we have now. But I was determined to save up the money to make this happen. Then, something life-changing happened a couple months later. I received the news that I was pregnant with twins! So the funds I had saved went to my babies. I put my search on the back burner and the years passed by.

As I stated in Chapter One, I decided to stand in my truth and find my birth mother in 2020. I purchased the Ancestry DNA kit and was so excited to finally find the missing pieces of my life. I sent in the kit and downloaded the app to keep me informed of the progress. Six weeks later, the results came in while I was in New Jersey celebrating Pia's 50th birthday. It was a very busy weekend, and I did not read the results until Sunday morning before I left to come home. As I read my results, I was floored to know I was related to over 1,000 people. I scrolled through the names, finding several second cousins.

One of their profile pictures caught my attention. We had the same eyes, cheekbones, dimples, and lips! It was crazy to see someone who looks similar to you. I continued to read, her name was Tiffany, and she was from Virginia! Remember I mentioned Virginia before? I knew she would be able to help me find my mother. I sent Tiffany an inbox, and she got back to me very quickly. I told her I was looking for my mother, and she was happy to help. We exchanged numbers, I told her my mother's name, and she said, "Yes, I know her; she is my cousin and my mother's first cousin." She called her mother and told her about me. She was just as shocked as I was, discovering that my mother never told anyone in her family that she had given birth to me. Remember, she was in New York at the time and did not go back home until after I was born. They informed me that I had a sister named Terresa who still lived in the same city that our mother was from. Sadly, my mother passed away in 2007.

Nevertheless, I was still happy to finally meet my birth family. Hopefully, she was happily looking down and seeing that I had finally come home. Tiffany gave me a number to my Aunt Sharon, my mother's brother's wife, who was able to really help me. After the initial shock, she was nice enough to go to her job and give Terresa my phone number. I asked Aunt Sharon not to tell her who I was but let her know that it was about her mother. Later that afternoon, I received a call from my sister. I said, "I don't know how to tell you this, so I'm going to just say it. I am your sister."

Terresa didn't say a word, then she started laughing. She shouted, "I always knew you were out there. I knew I was not crazy!" Finally, the mystery was solved. She continued to explain.

Easter of 1970, a picture was taken of my mother, sister, and brother. In the picture, my mother was pregnant with me. I was born in June of the same year. Years later, Terresa found the picture and asked my mother where the baby was. My mother replied, "Child, I was just fat." When my sister was 18 years old and now had a child of her own, she came across the picture again. She asked the same question knowing our mother was definitely pregnant.

Nevertheless, she stuck to the same story. But Terresa did not stop believing that she had a younger sibling somewhere in this huge world. At that point in our conversation, I was overwhelmed with emotions. I could not believe I was talking to my big sister! I sent her my adoption paperwork and my picture. She could not believe how much I looked like her, my brother, and "Ma." We stayed on the phone for hours, sharing information and getting to know each other.

As I was making connections with my new family, I reached out to another second cousin Terri who was very instrumental in the process. She responded quickly as well. We exchanged numbers, and she helped me navigate through the app. I thought she was one of my cousins on my mother's side; however, she was from my father's side. I was shocked because I did not have any information about my father, so I was not expecting to find him. Terri asked me some questions about my mother, and when she asked where she was from, her wheels started turning. Terri stated she had a cousin that was 96 years old and had a son who is the same age that I had on my paperwork. Terri said, "Let me make some phone calls. In the meantime, reach out to your mother's side of the family and give them his name to see if it rings a bell."

So I did. When I called back my Aunt Sharon and gave her the name, she screamed, "Yes, that has to be him! They were dating around that time." Seeing I am the second cousin to Terri, and that was her cousin, I knew that was my father. Now I needed to find how to get in contact with him. Well, Aunt Sharon to the rescue again.

Her hairdresser is my father's niece, so she contacted her. After explaining to my cousin the story, she called, and my father was at work. The next morning, she gave me a call with his phone number. I called and was so nervous I could not believe I was about to speak to my birth father.

After saying hello, he asked me one question. "Who is your mother?" I told him, and the next words he said was, "I am your father!" He told me how he was looking for me and actually went to The Oprah Winfrey show to ask for help. That is a good feeling to know someone in this world was out there looking for you. He always counted me in his kids' roll call. People always asked where is this oldest child. He said, "I don't know, but she is out there."

On my father's side, I have three sisters and one brother. So I went from being an only child to six siblings in a blink of an eye. What a change! Well, there you have it, my family connection. Something that took me so many years to do, and when I decided to complete the search, it only took one day to locate my birth parents. DNA is an amazing thing!

The Overwhelming Response

After connecting with my birth family, the news about me spread like wildfire. I received so many calls and texts welcoming me to the family from both sides of the family. It was overwhelming yet beautiful. I have to recognize my two nephews Antione Hall and LaRoy Morton, and niece Katrice Terry who took me in as their auntie from day one. I am now Auntie ReGina, and I love it. These people are my blood, who I actually have a biological connection with. Unfortunately, some people take that for granted. For many years, I only had my children as my only blood relatives. Now, I had physical roots, and the feeling was indescribable. I finally had people who looked like me, my mannerisms, and my traits. When I first saw my mother's picture, my mouth dropped! I saw myself all day long from the smile, dimples, nose, body shape, and after talking to my family, we sound, walk and act alike.

When I video chatted with my father the first time, I noticed I had his hands, eyes, and height. We both like nice things and being organized. I was also able to video chat with my 97-year-old grandfather! I looked at his hand, and I saw where my hands came from. When I was little, I noticed my left pinky finger was shaped differently than the other fingers. It looked like it had been broken and never healed correctly. My grandfather and my father have that same distinct pinky.

I never thought that this day would come that I would relate to people on this level. What many others take for granted, I cherish wholeheartedly. Having a blood connection with my birth family was one of my wildest dreams. And now God had brought it into fruition.

"In a study of American adolescents, the Search Institute found that 72% of adopted adolescents wanted to know why they were adopted, 65% wanted to meet their birth parents, and 94% wanted to know which birth parent they looked like."

(https://www.americanadoptioncongress.org/)

You can go to the ".gov" website of the state you were adopted in to get instructions on how to request your non-identifying info. It should provide a physical description of your birth parents as well as their education level and/or the type of employment they had.

(https://adoption.org/can-find-birth-family-little-information)

CHAPTER FOUR

I FOUND MY BIRTH FAMILY! NOW, WHAT?

The First Visits

Well, the time had come to meet my new family in person. I met my little sister Brittany, brother-in-law, and niece first, who came from Maryland. I was so excited that I rushed to the door as they were getting their things out of the car. In disbelief, I watched my sister walk up. COVID-19 had just rushed onto the scene when I found my family, and this was two months later. We followed the safety precautions; however, I had to hug my baby sister. We had a great couple of days getting to know each other. Being the only child, I never had nieces, nephews, or in-laws. So I enjoyed getting to know them. Next up was my father, Nathaniel, my stepmother Vanessa and my sister Monique, who came from Georgia. I had my son video record this event. I was so nervous my stomach had butterflies. When I heard them getting out of the car, I ran downstairs. My dad had a dozen of roses and a big smile on his face. We hugged for a while.

To finally meet in person and know this is the person that gave you life! Wow, the feeling was overwhelming. When I hugged my sister and really looked at her, I noticed we looked very similar. It was amazing! I had a new stepmother as well. Just seeing them in person was one of my greatest moments. While we were enjoying the weekend, my dad received a call that his sister, my aunt passed away. I could not believe this was happening. I was just getting to know him, but I wanted to support him the best I could. Then I began to think about it; this was the best place he could have been. He was with his wife and children. God made sure he was surrounded by love.

He was only two and a half hours away from his hometown, so he asked if I wanted to go with him to check on the family. Of course, I did! The next morning, we headed to the place my birth parents are from. As we were riding down, I sat next to my sister, and we talked. I still could not believe I was there with my newfound family. Oh, by the way, I did not mention that my other two sisters lived in

Danville, so I would meet them too. I had a mixed bag of emotions; however, I was more excited about meeting my sisters, aunts, uncles, nieces, nephews, and cousins.

Our first stop was at my sister Natalie's house. It was once again a great feeling to hug yet again another sister! She made us breakfast, and we talked and took some pictures. I also met her daughter, my niece. Next, we visited my aunt and then on to my uncle's house, where I met more of my family. Undeniably, it was wonderful meeting everyone. I told my sisters that I wanted to surprise my other sister on my mother's side Terresa because she did not know I was in Danville. While planning to surprise Terresa, my father, two sisters, and I went to the supermarket to buy some items. As we shopped, I heard a man call out my father's name, at the time not knowing he was my brother-in-law. All of a sudden, I saw this woman running towards me. Immediately, I realized it was my sister Terresa! We were screaming and hugging while the store employees wondered what was going on. Although it was not my plan, it was God's plan. She ended up surprising me. Now, I have met my father and four of my sisters. I have spoken to both of my brothers, and we will meet real soon. I can't wait! I have so many other family members to meet. As the world reopens from the pandemic, I will definitely be traveling and spending some quality time with them.

The New Normal

Now the introductions were done, and the next step is to get to know my new family. They are now included in my new normal. Being raised as an only child, I never had this experience of siblings and navigating through this process. Where do I begin in building these new relationships?

The best way to describe it is as giving birth. Most women experience labor pains and discomfort. However, after you see your child's face, all that pain goes out the window. My new family is the same. I don't care if we just met; I love each one of them unconditionally. I am learning that each person is different and has different journeys they are on. I just have to be there to support and love.

I have witnessed other brother and sister relationships all my life; however, it is different when experiencing it yourself. Since I have been absent from their lives for 50 years, I will be patient and empathetic.

I am looking forward to building our relationships and going to enjoy the journey. Getting to know my birth father has been amazing! We have a lot in common, and the conversations are wonderful as well. He calls me almost every day just to check on me. I had the pleasure of spending two weeks with him and his wife, so we are in a good place. I am blessed he is still here, and I can be in his life.

Unfortunately, my birth mother passed away before I was able to meet her. Of course, I was saddened to hear that she passed. Still, I believe she is and has been looking down upon us and is now happy her children are all together. As the family tells me all these great stories about my mother, I am amazed at how much we are alike. We have the same passion for giving back to the community. We believe in standing up for ourselves and helping others in need. My nephew said we even walk and sound the same. Every time I met a new family member, they were taken back by how much I look and sound like her.

Isn't that amazing how you never met a person and can have the same traits and mannerisms? Since I cannot build an earthly relationship with her, I wanted to show her that I appreciate the sacrifice and unconditional love she had shown me. With the help of my sister, brother, niece, and nephews, we held a beautiful rededication ceremony to honor her. All the family came to the gravesite to celebrate this great woman. Even the city of Danville recognized her as well. I was able to get a scholarship in her name and presented it to my sister. I felt this was the least I could do for the woman who gave me life and a chance to make a mark in this world. I am so grateful that my new family has welcomed me with open arms. As soon as the world opens back up, we plan to have the grandest family reunion ever, bringing all sides together.

LOOKING FOR YOUR BIRTH PARENTS OR BIRTH RELATIVES?

"Child Welfare Information Gateway, a service of the Children's Bureau, Administration for Children and Families, offers a web section that outlines the search process's steps. The publication <u>Searching for Birth Relatives</u> contains basic information on obtaining birth and/or adoption records, conducting a search, reuniting with birth relatives, dealing with the lifelong emotional impact of adoption, and links to relevant organizations."

Source - https://www.acf.hhs.gov/cb/faq/

CHAPTER FIVE

WISDOM KEYS

Proverbs 3:5–6 (NKJV):

Trust in the LORD with all your heart,
And lean not on your own understanding;
In all your ways, acknowledge Him,
And He shall direct your paths.

❖ Being adopted is being blessed four times. If you use the right mindset, you will see that you were chosen four times by God.

❖ God's plan is always the right plan. Don't be ashamed about being adopted. Trust in God's divine order. Remember, you had no choice or say in this decision.

❖ Family is important. However, we are not promised perfection. Learn to love yourself and love them for who you are together.

❖ Whatever you decide to pursue in life, put God first, and He will guide you every step of the way. But let me warn you! There will be unknown blessings along the way that are going to blow your mind. I am excited about your future!